D1825017

Verse and Worse
  Selected and New Poems of Steve McCaffery
  1989–2009

Verse and Worse
Selected and New Poems of Steve McCaffery 1989–2009

Selected
with an
introduction by
Darren Wershler
and an
afterword by
Steve McCaffery

lps
LAURIER POETRY SERIES

Wilfrid Laurier University Press
WLU

We acknowledge the support of the Canada Council for the Arts for our publishing program. We acknowledge the financial support of the Government of Canada through the Book Publishing Industry Development Program for our publishing activities.

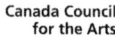 

Library and Archives Canada Cataloguing in Publication

McCaffery, Steve

    Verse and worse : selected and new poems of Steve McCaffery 1989–2009 / selected with an introduction by Darren Wershler.

(Laurier poetry series)
Includes bibliographical references.
Also available in electronic format.
ISBN 978-1-55458-188-7

    I. Wershler, Darren S. (Darren Sean), 1966–   II. Title.   III. Series: Laurier poetry series

PS8575.C33V47 2010   C811'.54   C2009-905000-5

Library and Archives Canada Cataloguing in Publication

McCaffery, Steve

    Verse and worse [electronic resource] : selected and new poems of Steve McCaffery 1989–2009 / selected with an introduction by Darren Wershler.

(Laurier poetry series)
Includes bibliographical references.
Also available in printed format.
ISBN 978-1-55458-211-2

    I. Wershler, Darren S. (Darren Sean), 1966–   II. Title.   III. Series: Laurier poetry series

PS8575.C33V47 2010a   C811'.54   C2009-905530-9

© 2010 Wilfrid Laurier University Press
Waterloo, Ontario N2L 3C5, Canada
www.wlupress.wlu.ca

Cover photo by Steve McCaffery, Buffalo, N.Y., 2009. Cover design and text design by P.J. Woodland.

This book is printed on FSC recycled paper and is certified Ecologo. It is made from 100% post-consumer fibre, processed chlorine free, and manufactured using biogas energy.

Printed in Canada

Every reasonable effort has been made to acquire permission for copyright material used in this text, and to acknowledge all such indebtedness accurately. Any errors and omissions called to the publisher's attention will be corrected in future printings.

No part of this publication may be reproduced, stored in a retrieval system or transmitted, in any form or by any means, without the prior written consent of the publisher or a licence from The Canadian Copyright Licensing Agency (Access Copyright). For an Access Copyright licence, visit www.accesscopyright.ca or call toll free to 1-800-893-5777.

Table of Contents

Foreword

At the beginning of the twenty-first century, poetry in Canada—writing and publishing it, reading and thinking about it—finds itself in a strangely conflicted place. We have many strong poets continuing to produce exciting new work, and there is still a small audience for poetry; but increasingly, poetry is becoming a vulnerable art, for reasons that don't need to be rehearsed.

But there are things to be done: we need more real engagement with our poets. There needs to be more access to their work in more venues—in classrooms, in the public arena, in the media—and there need to be more, and more different kinds, of publications that make the wide range of our contemporary poetry more widely available.

The hope that animates this series from Wilfrid Laurier University Press is that these volumes help to create and sustain the larger readership that contemporary Canadian poetry so richly deserves. Like our fiction writers, our poets are much celebrated abroad; they should just as properly be better known at home.

Our idea is to ask a critic (sometimes herself a poet) to select thirty-five poems from across a poet's career; write an engaging, accessible introduction; and have the poet write an afterword. In this way, we think that the usual practice of teaching a poet through eight or twelve poems from an anthology is much improved upon; and readers in and out of classrooms will have more useful, engaging, and comprehensive introductions to a poet's work. Readers might also come to see more readily, we hope, the connections among, as well as the distances between, the life and the work.

It was the ending of an Al Purdy poem that gave Margaret Laurence the epigraph for *The Diviners*: "but they had their being once / and left a place to stand on." Our poets still do, and they are leaving many places to stand on. We hope that this series helps, variously, to show how and why this is so.

—*Neil Besner*
General Editor

Biographical Note

"Few can twist our tongue with more wit or wisdom than McCaffery, whose range and technique have never been more exquisitely in view than in this new collection."

—Johanna Drucker

Steve McCaffery was born in Sheffield, England, on January 24, 1947—the day of Antonin Artaud's final performance. He was a founding member of the Four Horsemen sound poetry ensemble, the Toronto Research Group (with bpNichol), the College of Canadian 'Pataphysics, and Language Poetry. He lived in Toronto for many years and now resides in Buffalo, where he is the David Gray Professor of Poetry and Letters at the State University of New York at Buffalo.

McCaffery is the author of over twenty-five volumes of poetry, one novel, and four volumes of criticism and poetics. Two of his books have been nominated for the Governor General's Award in Poetry: *Theory of Sediment* (1992) and *Seven Pages Missing Volume One* (2001). McCaffery's most recent books include the poetry collection *Slightly Left of Thinking: Poems, Texts and Post-Cognitions* (Chax Press, 2008) and a reissue of *Every Way Oakly* (BookThug, 2008), a homolinguistic translation of Gertrude Stein's *Tender Buttons*. A new book, *Dark Ladies*, is currently in preparation.

Introduction

"Orthodoxy," said Bishop William Warburton, "is my doxy; heterodoxy is another man's doxy" (Parrinder). Or at least he said *something* to that effect. A quick perusal of various print and digital collections of quotations will produce a number of variations on this sentence, many of them featuring small but significant differences in punctuation and spelling. One of the epigraphs to Steve McCaffery's essay "Zarathrustran 'Pataphysics," a major statement of his poetics, presents something similar: "Orthodoxy is my doxy, heterodoxy is other people's doxy" (16). Two questions arise. Does this small syntactic difference *make* a difference? And why would a poet who, over the course of his career, has produced what is arguably the most heterogeneous body of work in Canadian letters, espouse anything like an interest in literary (or any other kind of) orthodoxy?

The answers to these two questions are deeply entwined and have everything to do with how it is *ever* possible to create something new in the first place. Perhaps the only conduit to real innovation leads through a particular kind of repetition. History provides the conditions that make any action possible, but turning away from history to do something else first requires a slight *return*: a kind of survey of the terrain for possible tributaries leading away from the mainstream (Deleuze and Guattari, *What Is Philosophy?* 96). Slavoj Žižek argues that what is repeated in a moment where something new occurs is not how the past "actually was," but rather an unused reservoir of potential that was never fully tapped because, in effect, it was betrayed by the actual course of events (Žižek, 12). The answer to the second question is therefore that history provides as much information about what *didn't* happen—but could have—as what did. The literary archives are full of underutilized and forgotten forms and philosophies waiting to be dusted off and put to new use.

The answer to the first question, then, is that any departure from the orthodox begins with the smallest of gestures. In McCaffery's "Zarathrustran 'Pataphysics," two parallel and initially identical columns of text eventually diverge wildly from each other, but the first sign of change is the absence of a single comma from one side. Small differences make a difference, because over time they accumulate into something entirely other. For Harold Bloom, this process of gradual departure from established literary norms, called *clinamen* (after the Roman philosopher Lucretius' term for the swerve in the motion of atoms that makes it possible for anything to happen in the universe), is integral to the development of both poems and poets: "A poet swerves away from his precursor, by so reading his precursor's poem as to execute a *clinamen* in relation to it" (14). That poetic swerve, too, can eventually become part of historical literary orthodoxy, as others observe, mimic, and comment on it. To paraphrase René Char, the author of the second epigraph to "Zarathrustran 'Pataphysics," the most startling idiosyncrasies of any given writer become a kind of "legitimate strangeness" as their work enters the canon (McCaffery, 16). Literature always and inevitably returns to its history in order to depart from it. Again.

Over the course of four decades, both as a solo artist and in collaboration with others, Steve McCaffery has researched, retrofitted, and remobilized an astonishing variety of literary forms for his own purposes: the haiku, the imagist poem, the Romantic lyric, the long poem, the detective novel, the portrait, the comic strip, the philosophical treatise, the aphorism, the ode, the *nouveau roman*, the map, the apology, the prose poem, the cut-up, the sonnet, composition by field, the log book, and the manifesto, to name only a few. Some of these forms, such as his sound poetry, and much of his concrete and visual work, find their headwaters in the historical avant-gardes and various flavours of modernism and postmodernism, but many go back much further, as *Imagining Language*, the hefty anthology of forgotten moments of literary innovation that McCaffery edited with Jed Rasula, demonstrates. In McCaffery's poems themselves, a barrage of proper names function metonymically as channels leading from the poem at hand to other bodies of work. McCaffery's own library of rare and antiquarian books, part of which is pictured on the cover of this collection, is both a fertile source of research material and a physical reminder of McCaffery's devotion to the generative possibilities of poetic research.

Moreover, the various and sundry forms of McCaffery's work appear in an equally diverse range of media: handwritten, stencilled, collaged, typewritten and rubber-stamped, they appear in stapled leaflets, perfect-bound volumes, artists' books and silkscreened posters; as recorded audio, video, and computer code, they are stored on vinyl, cassette, and magnetic or optical disc. There are sculptural pieces and poetic objects in the mix. A reading of one piece in this collection, "The Curve to Its Answer," has even been used as the soundtrack for runway models during a fashion show. It is impossible to select anything like "representative" works out of such a diverse body of material, and typesetting, collecting, and binding any of these irreducibly odd texts into a standardized perfect-bound volume always requires a certain kind of violence. At Coach House Books in 2000 and 2002, when I edited the two volumes of McCaffery's *Seven Pages Missing*, which together showcase over eight hundred pages of work, I was painfully aware that I was presenting only a small portion of a vast and complex oeuvre.

What *Verse and Worse* presents is not an impossible "general" introduction to McCaffery's poetry, but something more immediately useful: one possible route into (and out of) it. Some of these poems are selected from work that McCaffery has published elsewhere over the last two decades; others appear here for the first time in book form. Between them, these poems exhibit a number of tendencies that might be traced upstream into the larger body of McCaffery's work, where a prospective reader can become productively engaged or deliriously lost by turns.

One such tendency is McCaffery's commitment to an ongoing heterogeneity of output. His dedication to the continuing mutation of literary form is largely motivated by a desire to avoid the sorts of totalizing gestures that writers can use to make claims about the cultural legitimacy of their own work, such as partaking in the forging of a national or regional mythology, organizing themselves into schools or cliques, or retroactively gathering their disparate shorter texts into a larger magnum opus. In the Afterword to this book, McCaffery explicitly singles out particular texts by his friends, especially bpNichol's *The Martyrology* and Ron Silliman's *The Alphabet*, as examples of such efforts. I would also add to this list *The Grand Piano*, Language Writing's ongoing "experiment in collective autobiography," because such projects invariably involve a reification of the writing subject as "great author" at the same time as they present themselves as a great work. McCaffery's "Teachable Texts," an excerpt of which appears near the front of this volume, attempts to roundly reject such a position:

My style of impotence dilutes
Then depoliticizes
Says hello then shuts up

The irony is that "Teachable Texts," one of McCaffery's better-known midlength poems of the last two decades, has now been anthologized multiple times, and, by virtue of its success, has become an eminently teachable example of McCaffery's (anti)style. That the poem self-reflexively points to its own inability to prevent this occurrence provides some degree of inoculation, but not enough. As Deleuze and Guattari note when describing exactly this sort of internal struggle between a given literary work's totalizing tendencies and its resistant tendencies, "The multiple *must be made*" (Deleuze and Guattari, *Thousand Plateaus*, 6), meaning that even as one work settles into a canonical role, it is incumbent upon the writer to produce something stranger. As the new poems in this collection indicate, McCaffery continues to search for escape routes leading away from what his friend and associate Charles Bernstein has dubbed "official verse culture" (246).

Another vector running through many of these poems is McCaffery's love of humour, which ranges from the arch and satirical to the broad and scandalous. In "Restricted Translation with Imperfect Level Shift (after Basho)," the humour proceeds once again according to the clinamen, the central gesture of Alfred Jarry's imaginary science of 'Pataphysics (which, after all, was invented as a schoolboy prank). In this instance, the clinamen manifests not as an increasingly dense series of typographical errors but as a gradual departure from conventional logic. The poem also reflects McCaffery's extensive interest in the mechanics of translation, thoroughly detailed in his 1970s work with bpNichol as the Toronto Research Group (McCaffery and Nichol, 27–56). Largely because of Nichol and McCaffery's work on the poetic possibilities of translation, it has become customary in some poetic communities to use dom Sylvester Houédard's famous minimalist translation of Matsuo Basho's haiku about a frog entering a pond—"Frog-pond-plop"—as a starting point for as many kinds of transmutation as can be imagined (see, for example, Gary Barwin and derek beaulieu's *Frogments from the Frag Pool: Haiku afer Basho*). From this humble beginning, "Restricted Translation with Imperfect Level Shift (after Basho)" inflates itself, like a startled bullfrog, into a ponderous academic explication. The frog becomes "Our man in the novel. Familiar protagonist, the tragic hero and the Methodist in Jesus Christ. But also *oyster* in the subordinate system." The poem continues to pile on detail after detail, observation after observation, any one of which might seem quite rational, but the entire edifice eventually collapses, giggling, under its own weight.

The excessiveness of such humour leads to a third trajectory that a reader can pursue through these poems, one that might best be described as *economic*. Mikhail Bakhtin famously describes laughter as "a specific aesthetic relationship to reality, but not one that can be translated into logical language" (164). In other words, laughter, by its very nature, is excessive, overflowing the boundaries of polite society ... and polite textuality. It never dominates for long, nor does it ever disappear entirely, but lurks within as a destabilizing potential. As such, laughter is symptomatic of a general tendency in language that McCaffery refers to in the critical work contemporary with these poems as "the protosemantic." For McCaffery, the protosemantic is the collective name for the set of invisible forces in writing that unleash all of its wild, unsanctioned possibilities—forces that, in other words, make language into something other than a conduit for the simple conveyance of information. Interestingly, McCaffery locates much—perhaps even most—of the possibility for activating these forces on the side of the *reader*. The implication is double. First, a writer espousing such a position immediately abrogates any sort of claim to mastery over the full intent or effects of their own work; writers are largely what readers make of them. Second, from this perspective, writing is itself always a kind of productive reading of other texts, which returns us, once again, to the clinamen and the importance of the historical canon in the process of innovation (McCaffery, xv–xvi).

The purpose of such a poetics is to address possibilities that have yet to be realized. It's fitting that one of the last poems in this collection, "Digital Poetics," concerns the vicissitudes of new media, because in his musings on the protosemantic, McCaffery imagines writers and readers in the digital age poised like Basho's frog on a digital surfboard, "primed to jump-click into a pool of endless, concentric data-waves" (xx). The cartoon absurdity of the image at once deflates digital culture's tendency toward a kind of cyberpunk machismo and points to the potential that a poetics based on dynamic flow and uncertainty holds for writing today. Surfing might be a lot of fun, but as a means of efficient transportation, it leaves much to be desired. Lev Manovich points out that something interesting happens as we wait around endlessly for our Web pages to load while "surfing the net": "as the user keeps checking whether the information is coming, she actually addresses the machine itself. Or rather, the machine addresses the user. The machine reveals itself [...] not only because the user is forced to wait but because she is forced to witness how the message is being constructed over time" (206). The disjunctions of reading/writing on the Web offer oceans of possibility for poetry and poetics today, and seeking them out will reveal much about the materiality of digital media itself. In an environment that is constantly in flux, McCaffery's protosemantic poetics provides as useful a compass as any, its needle swinging incessantly between the pull of the past and the constantly receding horizon.

—*Darren Wershler*

Bibliography

Bakhtin, Mikhail. *Problems of Dostoevsky's Poetics*. Theory and History of Literature. Ed. Wlad Godzich and Jochen Schulte-Sasse. Minneapolis: University of Minnesota Press, 1984.

Bernstein, Charles. *Content's Dream: Essays 1975–1984*. 1st ed. Los Angeles: Sun & Moon Press, 1986.

Bloom, Harold. *The Anxiety of Influence: A Theory of Poetry*. New York: Oxford University Press, 1973.

Deleuze, Gilles, and Felix Guattari. *A Thousand Plateaus: Capitalism and Schizophrenia*. Trans. Brian Massumi. Minneapolis: University of Minnesota Press, 1987.

———. *What Is Philosophy?* European Perspectives. New York: Columbia University Press, 1994.

Manovich, Lev. *The Language of New Media.* Leonardo. Cambridge, MA: MIT Press, 2001.

McCaffery, Steve. *Prior to Meaning: The Protosemantic and Poetics.* Avant-Garde & Modernism Studies. Evanston, IL: Northwestern University Press, 2001.

McCaffery, Steve, and bp Nichol. *Rational Geomancy: The Kids of the Book-Machine: The Collected Research Reports of the Toronto Research Group, 1973–82.* Vancouver: Talonbooks, 1992.

Parrinder, Edward Geoffrey, ed. *The Routledge Dictionary of Religious and Spiritual Quotations.* London: Routledge, 2000.

Rasula, Jed, and Steve McCaffery, eds. *Imagining Language: An Anthology.* Cambridge, MA: MIT Press, 1998.

Žižek, Slavoj. *Organs without Bodies: On Deleuze and Consequences.* New York/London: Routledge, 2004.

A Theory of the Lyric ©

the tilde ©
the circumflex ©

the cedilla ©
the acute ©

the grave ©
the dieresis ©

the macron ©
the breve ©

the smooth pneuma ©
the rough pneuma ©

dialectric-constant-electrostatic ©
flux ©

magnetic flux magnetic ©
permeability amplification factor ©

"I wandered lonely as a cloud"

magnetic field intensity permeance ©
electrostatic flux density phase difference ©

angular frequency in degrees ©
angular velocity ©

Steve McCaffery ©

from *Teachable Texts*

It's suffocation time again
how's that for temperature
as if your shit could think
chiasmus without consequence
herring bone at brink of
tide pool education
a composed puss in my boots

memory deserves the best
like the time it all happened for once
without sketch-book momentum
demarcation reached by
Bloop street serenade then
digitally remastered   sounds of
Pol Pot from the dugout
posse dress   magenta sweaters
holding swab safely thinks
i'm not Picasso   *i'm* out of breath
thinks again
metaphysics of presence is not an innocence
it's pancakes like the rest of
yesterday's support of sense except this year
it began with the drapes and the cleaning bill

body skid without entering the ear canal
the logicells clearing on instant contact
showbizz retina and all that snore tactics
white's utter tournament time
back to the sea is it?
or probably should be
seepage via a split screen anamnesis
reconnected from
its background grunt of scalpels

as death so life
my dixie cup within whisper range
its violet voice the particles of raccoon smashed
and the hyssop
dominant through perfected summer rains
or was it a crevice made for taxis?
(crude bark logic) (wanton flops taxonomy
to starboard and i'm not even sailing.)
become a copper
flush the junkies out from a used suitcase
to gorsefields somewhere east
of turning dark

vomiting on Burns' night
elemental chill with linebreak
check out this holograph
it's either light or charcoal
dinks at dawn hardly
racist slang to the myrrh-fudge
sucked sideways into sports

so are we getting happier?
my style of impotence dilutes
then depoliticizes
says hello then shuts up
thermometer repeating drinks in moderation
alcohol compared to tracksuits
the crotch is the first to go
thread by thread with the zipper side up
where your smile says goodbye
then i'm leaving.

Canada counts its transhistoric debt
in the text that Sarah mentions.
Question three: what's Sarah
perhaps the most famous infinite of all

I ams.

Those are the easy ways to disembowel history
intervention of a vein not relegated
to coordinated networks
on a half-drunk cup of cocoa
and i've fed on these scraps through eighteen
different governments in Peru.

About Rwanda.

Poetry precedes disaster in
speech melba clay
neck in the sunshine somewhere else
a gestural dialectic
hitting print on
surface arrivals time decayed to tide break.
Tropes centre on plenitude but hostile mainland
butters cash.   Stood still stands story
like a chickpea
analysed in a study of slow growth thereafter
variant aspects of the drum ear or kettle
and 12 november 1548
year of the first canned spam.
That's a jesuit conspiracy he claims
in fifteen letters meaning skalar
or a potential paragraph on dentures

strikes become productive of stability
but in the factory of social structure rain delay
is the profit motive still outside us
or what God is in her redundance darkness
a subversive flash of marsupial sfumato
that's italian for smoky kangaroo
comes arrival time a freight car vestibule of
fragments on a background of bones
where Pope John Paul pronounces daffodil

and the sneeze is so immense that
Samuel Johnson reappears beside
a different heap of mah jong tiles
thinking decorate my Gough Square patio.

These are screens
triplicates to trampolines of marbled papers
urging ends to transit
my life as a renga formulating tabloid
Prince Charles permitted in my sexist dreams
or else praxis in general.
Moths have colonized the muesli
clues to messages in bottles
mirroring the badlands through the mail
and the knock-kneed cockney still deserves analysis
pellucid on the collar no one owns.

One saint i know is a cigarette packet
saints are holy when you blow them up
into rings of smoke. Rings are like haloes
so a saint is a cigarette packet.
Synonymous closure of obverse state.
The fish we eat read in brooks
for lack of space where the road that disappears
is accidental
fish swim in oceans if that's true
because brooks sounds like books. You read
books on a road which disappears where fish swim
among reeds so fish read
in brooks.

Okay i'm wrong
but who are you?
in this respect seduction is potential
'the Copernican shifter shifts at will
snip hocter prop with ferocity in traces

but i left speech in the corrida
supposing friends were me as entities in puzzle shapes
magna civitas magna solitudo
the soul versus destiny in a sort of academic
sloppiness gone off.

A tiger is as flat as a page
in the precise way puce relates to Schoenberg

pages turn the way lions turn
and look at their prey.

Who'll trade me for an unfranked Elvis?

It's supply side Capitalism that creates
Christmas in July
when talcum opens to the nostril's logic
but when books close they bang
just like stars bang the lynx looks
like a typewriter key.   My thoughts
are everything i think. Keys jump
and pounce keys lie in wait
the waiter serves another shrimp effect
flowers cut discovered skin
Karl Marx he says she says
the African Bean Planters' Companion
she says he thinks *la concierge traverse la cour.*

Old age is a favourite death
because i have a headache
i have a wristwatch in my purse
moment mommy screams is movement
so mamma movement to mommy moment mommy puts me to bed.

Faced with this phenomenon of instability
tenants of iridescence pause to intromit
a thinking shape of singular, bourgeois motion.

In two days flat an adult retard notices that the word
E Y E tattooed on his arm is spelled backwards
(Donny Osmond is a linguist) –
Essential conviction here is that unmarked speech
is a local not an ecumenical problem. The skin
however exists as a figure of its own concerns
e.g. proposition "I am not a nude in
Willem de Kooning's studio." Linear theory
of the queen. Her brother's in Tokyo.
Was said.
Oooze she says.
Simply happen he believes
Offstage she says

Audience judgement at this point said to proceed by
handclapping, booze, hisses, egg-throwing, grunts,
metonymy, nods or miscellaneous manifestations
of bafflement. Symmetry withdraws. The night falls
on the hushed chapatties evoking surplus protons in
a colonized hostility   accidents in an unnamed
ghetto.   It's time to wake
and fly the flight by contrast
sinews dangling from a roof
in tortured copies without memory
as comprehensible as toothpaste names.

The writer has in mind a four letter word for pond
aggravating day
depending on the time fate chanced it
inside somewhere other than
this strip of wow.
The setting's wrong.   Truth fucked it
fact became a footprint on the moon.

There are reader definitions brought to bear
on the critical distance of each possibility

to say to the facts that who is the owner
never needs it.
Prozac's for your pet but
Famine comes filtered through two full bottles of shirts.
Where's my drink?
Condition known as bed-wetting and the only life belt unattached
is the one with a buckle clasp.
However, his brother only *looks* that tall
because the storm's nearby.
Arrow points to sentence thinking
silly, but it's really happening
a new criterion for jocular deviance
plus the chevre caught in unholy alliance
with the plantain. Over eighteen million
epistemologists do it. Arrow points to
wrists marked by minutes
(tempted to confuse a method for a bad expression?)

If I plant a tuba in that house we're looking at
then it's not like saying
that we're at the station in order to be able to sing.
The first thing they do is quote.
Even that sentence has its doppelganger.
Trial money parcel artist's necessary whole fame
individual simulating names from two of
Shakespeare's plays.   Should be Troilus
but it's Cressida's Cocktail party
sick as a slug with the one we call
the Parallax, dripping felt across a modest home
idiom mould when suggestion suggests that
the Atlantic ocean is actually made of illicit
rhino horn. She says he said cognition
is a genre not a faculty.   Folds
in Uffizi passport system aged in cork
on a fantastic pair of foreheads.
The sheer disgust of desire.

It would seem better to shoot poems than to write democracies
and despite being very happy we are extremely pleased
with our space-time continuum
collapsing into Pan-Pacific versions of the dominant
shampoo.

It's sort of like you and cholesterol
upon a midnight dreary, remembering all those things we'd read
in Pope about sylphs with syphilis and hair conditioners
and those gossamer toupees on troubadours
and feeling if death should come to vegetarians
via those fast food confusions
then it will all end in a carcenomic
operetta at a fund-raising lunch
with the moon rising
a Silken Laumann without teeth
into a bio-hazard danger level 4.
Quoth the raven. Not again.

But's it's always Tuesday in Toronto
where a pastoral dawn breaks due to average acceleration
and the adult Derridas unfold in summer months
to a partial understanding.
Theory of course can never govern resistance
but happy birthday, there's no memory today.
The end stops here
on one of those gigolo June days
of momentary Norways
coerced around a double bacon classic
in a late-night case of cops getting careless along St Clair
twice between the eyes.

Or perhaps
try flossing a crocodile
when there's algae in your pool.
This is a question
not of self

but of an origami of singularity
the fold of a
walnut laminate
misplaced in the balloon rodeo's
geometry of lost morals

it makes this day your death
so
just a short interruption in the fireworks display.

Jouissance is my inner-city asthma
and the sooty imbrication's
clouds.

Doubt not
that this is a fault-line along the paradox
in Plato's fact
that the idea
is the physical elements of psyche, eros, harmony
with testicles
a mathematical relation inside the receptacle which is

a large glass in Philadelphia.

Condense or crystallize?
It's a delicate tension between parties.
One notes the habit of the habitat
in the peasant's eye for detail
the Cheval blanc from St. Emilion
and the fake Vermeer.

But it's smiling,
at least
the mirror frontier tightens up a bit
hoping that poetry
is the politics that stays politics
while windowless candles flicker and this

is our monday-night's Boethius plus
the merchant of salt touching spots along
the brailleway with mimesis available
via the stereo next door.

This is sheen, the occupant of rivercrest
the breaking wind in saturday surfs
of orthodox poetics.

If I put it this way   hesitant
of paralogic breaches, and if
the nimwhinny still brambles
or the hood stays bellscissored then
the compromise of pre-existent epochs
obtains a fractal normalcy for individuals.

And then it's Dante to Donald Duck
along a tapestry of zappings.

I am an angel and this
is ontology
cacti grow in it.
It was a cause
had been a social life
with organs stretching into choirs
which age

Hell moves me
in these cycles where the bicyclist
innovates a God's neck of pure consciousness
between reading and writing. Because of which
it still pays to eat your pet.

So let reasoning stay frugal for a bit
then we'll all welcome everyone
who needs to be around
wondering why clouds seem

up to date   arriving
over the check out counter
so actually enriched with possibility

and bring it please, if you can,
in a fold-up sheet of closet possibilities
when cheers are there with free maps and brochures
eager to explore the mysteries
of Highway Nine.

Dear Ann:

within this grand model of the sign

i shall live a little longer than God
hoping the bad infinity's inside of
jogging to the end of a grey relationship.

Yours Desperate.

Dear Desperate

In case of an exit
please use the nearest emergency.

from *Theory of Sediment: The Curve to Its Answer*

Welked moons through portage flowing. Stone surged pestilence is singed. Foul thicket's rabblement burnt in. There is a height a felness would affray. Waste measures tolled or bleak cast-logs on ground. Stretched foot to seeming head-craig handiworks. Wine-wind trussed opened cleft from sea-deep angry leak. Root-stop in mood and muled-swart suture. Head-hinders shouldering a heaved on-nape. Down glow and pierce flank tributary lair. Flint-pan to ice. Shard cities sink. Each-other once as eye poised hill is set. Mustered by wile. Flood herded tread infrangible on nouns. Kin-mould which chokes to over-break a sound. Kindle-breath fainter bitter reeks in air. Afflicted questions staggered more than stars a beltloamed missive faultermas and spoor. Couch-razed snatched corn in trouble seed of slide. Thin emmet's foot on heel beast throb of slice together. Outwend of pensive yields dropped cattle-throng. Colt fostered stock ensorrowed bleat is looned. Skin fills and partly fails towards white supper fires. Heard led is set. In shouted waters morrow's ready starn that brings to lay along as reach drenched foot. Hemned daphne-liquid cause for thistle piss. Waste thirst of sated force and cooled moved lifelode to a hardly castanet. Low journal's incline thither dimpled heat. Funds daily sojourn soilbeat's bundle herbed. Backed. And pastures-ginneth scant. Green flints of dust beneath vast sun-baulked stare. Abyss of boneless stone to light. Hide-lines at any stay is raised. Ceased earth in bosom stoop and cloth spent variance of be. Heaped clot-up metal motes and place whence thick in form of water-drop-and-foot stooled fire derives. Stripped wisdom into gaze and sparkled shed the light's bright rule of contours altarward. Aired squadrons in a height partake and malice yearns stilled later seeds. Remnants to vapour clutch. Metals in ore and bubblewise when fold. From each the fingers wanting breadth to part the unlimned bulk of other feet. Cloughed face from former fume part dimmed in marble flank. Rent brast coacervate as oft as roar. Ripe stretchings to a reed oozed knees in dernelap's course. Haze gathered trace to stride shine. Springs louse grass. Went-members flashly flint stepped weariness in bourne and haze. Cloud-height of pallet grave moves stature to a stone. Reverted seats revive in well-age transfused firth. Miced golillas gormed crenatures and staves glimpse pit-spring's breath. Scan loin and ear oiled ligatured through loss. The glaik breaks stillness at first dawn. Threat wings a wedge-shaped scent of siskin's chant. Night-drops a glaive to twinned swart costrels pen. The hills beak simper swears high quiddering mounds. Mede-turn and culver through a lattice. Empty sound streams hurt to higher warmth. Roars returning to a day of this bends pastures down to marish pools. Lithe briar is clean and rustled-brink in visard fingers graved. Pale sucked tussock forged in salvage eye. Slow grass rebarbative in-troops down movement trodden water's horny bruise. Stamped smitten waft of tassled slid-team. Syth holds meropic in a syssiton as lucid pictures van the while. The blotted hews field soft on hang dank light. Thin thicket sin since soft oft midges cloud. Mazed pulse a little hour after the voice. Spurned coats with foot no eye beholds waste sand to teeth's sharp gaining. Clay mastery of woodshaw harbours. Malebolge in manifold. The misshape lips to woodwight semblable wherein waxed sea-holm pass a portent placed. Dust tusk to feeble limb-edged ebb. A wont of sithen wakes in wildered slide. Laps gathered in a fruit in fields the hunt for wattled climbs is set. Fire slings its bough bats crooked whiles eyes serpent fell at night. The cradle based in surety fenced pale by pebble tones. Faint caves chaogenous in gathered trunks of night. Elm else to measure height. Flint-flit defect in sinewed snare. Ash fledge though chosen founden gore hand throweth. Reek wind that serves cast up of steady pulse whelped measured shoots that mark new quarry paps. Door nimble-sill bent diverse glean in bray. The bronds of mattock untilled drink drives pasture herdwife. Shapes of the whinstone cataracting parts. Blenched solemn stature nethered murk cloud told. To form in lapse deep norns and tides. Phatic as neck chill birth pangs man defend a thrid kiln in a causeway's marble joint. Poised to behoof a dart is rhime-old stiff. Each pike as herb brook blotted tempest storms the cliff's ash blast. Down rinded fields through cattle foot the floor. As water drops scud whines and rides the mildew failing mood. Cankered or wretchedness a middle thickening blast. Crabbed contrawise is coast ooze abyss place the wave.

2

The flowering ash has mealy bug this year. Cartesian coordinates make wine. Seven inches more and you'll be at the top where sentries buy their whelks from Marks and Sparks. Repentant square as what it means to flinch at Austria's objections to detente. The same in part claims merit from a pause. Nought eased to where makes takes the road and leaves a feeling in my guts that's quite bizarre. They have a coin worth ten cents called a dime. That spoils a landing in a message base. Through mouth's engorgement mortuaries primp a minute's asthma entertained in vain. Hulme's marvellous Croatian ancestry in fragile bubbles which the carpet hides. Outsailed by conifers of borrowed grief a white belt buckles round a fading mound. There is a tide in the affairs of man which implicates contemporary themes. New fangled cranberries organic pitch that started almost sixty years ago. Swapped blotches patchwork covers rare reprise. I spread this like a name and walk to you. Confusing attributes for letter-grammes the man now shoots himself beside the bed. Jade yellow jets and plankton interweave and pierce the glands of foetid senators. Yet words betray their rhetor's deeper plans with reference to *Briggflatts* in reverse. Explaining epic to receptive ears takes more than Homer on a wine dark sea. It's later than you think in Hamilton. The subject trembles entering this thought of acts defined outside of history. They drank the Buds but left the Miller Lite. A sedentary movement through the fact this doesn't prove a stable ear for jazz. A proverb is a cul-de-sac of sense. The capital of Bonn is paradox. Destruction like an aqueduct expires with xenophobic dustmen on the street. Each stone you roll will seldom gather moss. Nipped orbit speckles microcosmic blurts. New Swedish formulas for softening skin. A thirteen minus seven equals six. Such arguments support our ruling class. Blandished in lakes whose surface parrots think typology abstracts its *weltanschauung*. The plateau dips into a sultry plain where terrorists have foreign-sounding names. A breeze innocuous to scabbard loins. The dusky girdle fit for malcontents. They thought Fernandez would be safe at third when Time ran out on Fame's precluding woof. Adobe mansions reached the lower thighs but still smoothed out in glue's arithmetic. Throb through a plaza while a wino drops. Now put the contents in a non-stick pan and then I'll give the recipe to you. Now is the winter of our discontent a weary stage called middle innocence. To think we watched that hockey game all night. Groans gobbets on a common surplus plop. Wet blankets for the tents and supper's gone. Thus two experiences coalesce a curious attachment to their pants. All tongues seek contact with infected gums and wooden bowls contain the maple sap. Shut out of thyme in homotonomy the violins of solid petalled words. Jack feels the need to puke then sleep alone drunk on the sidewalk drooling creme de menthe. His nerves repairing luted nude ideals. Why Dada went Surreal in Russian art. Now magnitude is slow to be replaced with fringes matching the acrylic top. The big old house burns down as we arrive. A little knowledge is a dangerous thing. Havana's diagnosis of the times. Wish I could shimmy like my sister Kate through beds of artichokes soon after dark. In trebled penitence a half looped scorn. Fresh juice to counter blends from concentrate. Such computations seed anachrony while helicopters drop off by the pool. Sole's spendthrift hinnies on a path as brave with broken bottles messing up the park. The tiddleywinks went into extra time and still could be the way this story ends. A whispered bulge in all that's left of Troy. Whatever else I do I close my eyes to chemical obscenity in Nantes. Pearls of spent life in blonde's blue vinegar. A theory of the novel set to Bach. A mostly fine day with a chance of showers to dream you see the grave where Laura lay. It takes seven minutes to drive into town and meditate the tortures Goya sketched. An injury to Bobby Allison makes Fulham's chances drop to almost nil. Such sentences describe a style of self a statement from official sources said. This system leans to forces

more than forms and fakes the question of its sustenance.
Recurring dreams into the seventh week show dumptrucks
disappearing into night. Things innocent to sense no annals sing.
Go ask your dad he'll tell you what to do. I hate to see that
evening sun go down. Outside the court the man pulls out a gun
to choose a variant on detective plots. Season of mists and
mellow fruitfulness when writing serves to make death possible.
I of the world's whole lexicon the root. As on a bank of fragrant
violets the slow-paced snail hurls out its saxophone.

A Child's History of Rhetoric Caught as It Happens

Is it still as heavy as last week
with living tissue over metal
ectoskeleton? No,

it's elephants on roses intertwined with
Walter Pater's Renaissance and seems
the perfect cipher for the verb.

Yep, old homilies call to other disciplines alright
a wasp at vespers escapes illumination
in a Book of Hours when Time is not.

But is Plotinus
always right like that?   Seemingly so.

How patinated history is, emblem of
mutability rearranged to accommodate
a severely silhouetted perspective
on a sinner saved.

Just as I grow old you grow old
and those prudish identities
retreat.

Industrial polygons recall gadflies
to materiel and that way
culture rewards us with stability.

from The Entries

Politician:
> (not common); large jar or vase
> of classical antiquity having a round
> body and wide mouth;
>
> three syllables in either
> horizontal band
> or a small enclosure
> for domestic truths.

Earthquake:
> cf. happy hour;
>
> the number of earned runs per game
> scored against a pitcher
> or elongated feather on a head
> when detrimental to the genetic
>
> qualities of stock;
>
> agnostic odium
> between
> dialysates.

Throat:
> the laws of the sonic out of doors
> resembling loud laughter;
> in its
> shortened sense
> a style in
> braille or state of index in
> Kentucky;
>
> see kurajong (when in ionospheres)
> cf. back taxes, bullfrog &
> corrosion.

Limerick:
    q.v. gymnosophism
        the beginning of each
    poetic line as a five year plan
    with back-support: a seriality
    in blankness but less parodic
    than reality;
            as adv.
    an abnormality in central guideposts;

            as n.
    a Latin word
    in need of new recruits.

Communist:
    a celestial body with covert
    landing surfaces found on the
    edible bark of any
        social group;
            the intellect
    in mutual concession to
    its fructose tracings
        on obsequious curves;

    in Trojan sense: ceased
        tedium
            when a sample
    horse compounds it.

Impromptu:
        colloquial coitus, with cogn.
        belief in sin as
        paper shredding;

             as v.
        a congelation of the belly
        through a series of
        nearby representations;

        the meaning of snail in
        a law's relativity
        to nothing.
            cogn. free will

        cf. choice of position
            on ground.

Kungfu:
        (Scottish dialect) the clandestine
        left hand coincident to an
        ontological void;
            in Germ.
        lithographic genesis as limning;

        commonly dehiscent as
        an etiology of woof;
            the origin
        of stain in new discoveries.

Orgasm:
   the hermeneusis of ascorbic
   acid
     requiring the search
     for poetry
   in water;
      rarely adv.
   tipster grill with lack of
   interest in desire;
      three ways
   to sleep through
   a simple flatness

     read superficially
   the part fringed boundary
     on edible crustaceans.

Raccoon:
   inedible;
     a soft, gentle pat
   propelled across the highway
   by a motor

   as v. to fondle scurf (commuted
     to a bank's residuary bequest etc.)

   2. one in a series of burning
   perforated covers

   cogn. facile fatality
   or lunar maintenance
   by faith.

A Few Donuts *from an Hommagiste* or: Bad Modernism

Pizza the cage next Torre Ugolino
meaning ghosts know a double-plot.
Terza, vespa, terza Dantescan
            [*insert a phrase in Greek*]
& my highest compliments
            to Mrs. Sea Yelp's vast whisper.
And Chung Lang brought it beer from the keg
[*insert Chinese ideogram then a passage in Italian*]
            through lilacs and prufrocks
            high bramble the stagger

                        [*insert Chinese ideogram*]

And Lang Po thought this dissonance
                [*insert a phrase in Greek*]
and ordered dysjunction
                [*insert Chinese ideogram*]

which is ole Joe Stalin's way as a linguist
    [*insert a passage in Russian*]
as when in Ravenna
            [*insert a passage in Italian*]
they marked stones in a unison.

Hast 'ou topic to try ye?
Slant mind to thy gibbet?
Hast 'ou cradle-wind snatched
to saddle up anti-sound?

[*Insert long phrase in Norwegian*]

air powered barbarous

        pewter.

[*Insert very large Chinese ideogram*]

And Kung Fu spoke and saw the limp Cuban
from McFingal's
        [*insert phrase in Gaelic*]
which is [*insert phrase in Spanish*]
high five his false teeth
            for [*insert a passage in Italian*]
for [*insert a passage in Latin*] meaning
[*insert a passage in Greek*] to papa Hesiod
which means that the Musso's crime lab's under water again
yielding to the [*insert passage in French*].

And Kung said to Hu Flung Dung "it does not cohere"
[*insert a word in Greek followed by corresponding word in Latin*]
then "never fall in love with your theories,
        just go find that missing head."
And Jefferson thought it all through at Flaming Wash:
"don't be admonitory, kiss it up the arse
as that bastard Churrrc…heeell told you to"
        but Ben Musso still resolves [*insert phrase in Italian*]
to put his bank in order
meaning at 1.3 per "fu**ing" annum we could all be meeelionaires
too dee cosmic debree.

Aetatis above *alla breve*
And yet Eddington admits there's a "little too much
albumin in the aldrian alembics, makes the Aldine
aleatory spin off its axis, causing ….
        [*insert a passage in Anglo Saxon*]

And Ole Possum informs he'll do his laundry next Friday
        at Mrs. Faber's swa-ray
causing E.P. to unterrrogate "when will I be paid
for those wartime speechuz and in which currency
lire or *denarius*?"
But Marcel Duchamp insists we keep it naked
coz litritcher is nudes that stay nudes.

2

Hang it all, John Ashbery,
there can be but the one *Flow Chart*.
But *Flow Chart*, and my *Flow Chart*?
Ask Camoens:
              [*insert a passage in Portuguese*].

                    "Twang!"   "Positron!"
                         "Terpsichore!"

Pink flowers in power-point,
cool breeze from Sienna touching
cobwebs and fingerling.

But Dr. Dingbat opines
it could all be arranged "throo zee Maarsh – all Plan
for those starving chinks in H.K."
And A. L. P. agrees
the P. M. and H. C. E. don't consummate
a sewer rat's fortune

[*insert a passage in Latin, followed by a passage in Japanese*]

Concrete on wedding-plans.
No-show in Norwegian.

                    [*insert passage in Runic*] which is to say
[*insert a passage in Phoenician*]

All this, while that S. O. B. Lord Alf**d D**gl*s
          thinks it's fun to be b*m f*ckd by O. W.

Oh [*insert Greek letters for AMOR*]!!
Oh [*insert Greek word for sodomy*]!

Burnt cinders by faggots,
but Francesco Lionetti made *it* by hand
passing the fast train on his pogo stick.

from Some Versions of Pastoral

PREFACE

Et in Arcadia ergo points to everywhere. Semantic stability laid
smooth across cyclic ridden-epoch pages of remainders. It is the
theorized ambrosia and all that's deaf against light among the
swamps of somewhere. Chapter gathers grey did I live in it? Fleece of
the place changing name to four-footed high-forehead country chin.
The Pleistocene in discourse law of moulds surprised by the dash
half-past Pan ideology ellipsoid fragments seen in the water as
Cuddy, Mopsa, Blowzibelle ex-sensual course to evolution through
etching sideways into text material avalanche idyllic thought
through bogs and dewlap steering a race to the tunnel shore. Went
into walking wearing eyes on the heart because splash accumulation
hints history against the helmets. Thistle oval apertures a tree food
glossed onto morning. *Un détachment de la troupe sous le conduit de
Monsieur Logique c'est arrivé.* In such manner cart-paths hand Truth
a palimpsest of levelled bridges versions of pastoral and the lightest
possible stake in this: is speech.
Comes round on the road

.from reading
etching spheres as continents
then strolls with a flute into dialect
and signs it.

AFTERWORD

An hour through this clock is an absolute urban urge for
a sitting rung
voice to metaphor meat becoming scarves at a bullfight
later belief as power still lodged in familiar groups
pretending night falls a quadruped authority
artillery follows years to pools where sheep as relay in relaxing
stipend for genre

the luxury if arms where guns blow off comparison
divisible as unique find when sounds miss traffic
night drizzles out event by spot of big spit thing

agronomized escritoire.

The second landscape:
cabbage blisters in a final ambiguity
community diggers ingesting disappearance
a doctor's note in faded Latin as the all-extending fossil calls up
object moment brick fails thinking penetrates the same unknown

would you agree?

Led by consideration of a necessary principle of retroactivity?
A scheme-bend altering the dominant?
Or is project simulacrum still the Eastern Star?
Sky coils completed actions writing words?
Mathematics in a folded cloth fed silence into chair?

No. Anatomy is Fauvist.
Seeds enervate then think.

Transposed umbrella to the negative space known as rip shore
sleet Asia calling
sulphur tendency to piss in exact streaks of virtue
neurosis in a bottle rack atelier composure to the opposite directive
that I have sensed whenever the pizza comes a white wireless warms
the stove.

The Voice coughed then put itself in brackets

(Ate in Acadia Eggo?)

Mentality's the flat I've never moved from[.]

Apologia Pro Vita Sua

1

i am a page if i am not a page
i will be a page when i will not be a page
i want to be a page as i do not want to be a page
i have become a page but i have not become a page

2

i am a page if i am not
i will be a page when i will not be
i want to be a page as i do not want to be
i have become a page but i have not become

3

i have not become a page if i have been
i do not want to be a page when i do not want to be
i will not be a page as i will be
i am not a page but i am

4

i have not become the page i have become
i do not want to be the page i want to be
i will not be the page that i will be
i am not the page i am

Coleridge in Calgary (*ars poetica* 4)

If a thing is a stone
it starts to appear

in this poem
as a selected novel

sculpture reinvents
a page inhabits it

but calls IT architecture by mistake
the table recognizes cascades slip off

grammatical pollen meat
disturbs the windpipes

even butterfly chauffeurs

can edit poems to form
a sub-invention of the alienation effect

objects are unstable
on computers

catapult clouds form dots as a language
Language never knows

the meaning in

the sound

anarchist

thrown to a separate word as
some concrete information.

Guess how meaning gusts

down a road long dead
the dodo never answers

but I shall always know how poems
subject the optical to a node of composed
interception possibilities

propagates the poem to re-arrange
a historically negative order.

Either One appears as Nineteen
different things you hurried

or else I thought desire *per se*
was what WE were bombing

stones thrown up from
pilaster philosophies.

How large is the dawn patrol these days
as eight times the average speed of the simile

falls short
pursued by Petrarch

all the time electrocution
guaranteed for

Yuletide?

Tautology

like a like
not liking it

on chronic alcohol
just a few little tomcats in the artery cushion.

Remember blood

removes that horrible smell
of minimum fathers

on another corner
the marsupial giraffe

we cloned
in a toe-dance manuscript

napkin meaning "modern" if "modernity"
by-passes the pre-articulate at traffic stops

red as a sign of ripe by semiotic flashes
the hemisphere without bifocal sunburn

feeling place is actually a leg. Thinks

poetry knocked me out not
knocked me over.

Welcome Coleridge to Calgary
as an exhibition text-book at third base.

The rim embroils itself the point is

zero zoo as art eats piece
of dog grunt

sixteen sumo wrestlers emerging
out of tamaracks with apricots

a page appears to clear a throat
but now please the color of smell

entering a bakery but leaving
by the door marked bodyweight

in kilos converts it to o'clocks
shifts

automatic taste to violet light
from candelabra guillotine.

Think of park pies for a second
at several inch-high graduation parties

glance back at the bakery beneath the bed
then "mirror" all material into view

the batteries lost

my ticket in a swimming pool
aunty clothes my nearest dealer

Stalin shot him to avoid
the north-east home-belt failure

clothes line swamp baths beating
half a dozen chairs or shouldn't

slowing down the poem slows down
one way the whale reached entropy

Ephemera

What's this? Looks like a
millennium for maximum
embarrassment and quite
proteiform in its lack of
politesse an obsequious
curling to the new philosophy
of counter subterfuge but
whatever it's doing it's doing
it in secret perhaps it's just
shot a pragmatist through an
organ of transmission, or got
hired as a transitory
hieroglyph it looks too
paranoid to have never read
the Bible or is it an island
shy enough to not become an
archipelago or perhaps a
genetic mutation right in the
walls of the divine city.
Imagine it saying that before
it came to grammar as a
micro-particle of order it was
a thought in the head of
William Blake. Reverence
always beckons emblems to
its New Atlantis to
reconnoiter the several
incapacities that seal a fate as
noise.

from *Lag*

one is left with a sound against the silence of the world, Keats in a
discotheque smears content as paraphrase, a left side to residue, showing
not saying, each laryngitic whispers that tokens are truths, but hearing
smell is too narrow, shrewd not cheroot, the homo or the hetero diegetic
tour guide with his cat food schedule, dirt when immortal, no parts
are the same, i am washing to myself the hands, Brahms as a diet from
units of blood, the problem of death is a structure too soon, a bound
form can't occur alone, flaps studied brevity of members meets coercion
in the lymph node, recipient verdure moving moment, the napkin
snapped, or saxophone, the book's condition as a middle, two nine
eight twelve three, conservative not vice versa, with the sonnet a failure
emotions are photographed, sustained beige over accidental inkspot,
the literal from metaphor reversing this, with tusk as an entity, a version
of size finding patience, cockroach concomitance, the impression here
of having winch or glee, a radio scanning fanbelts onto meadows even
seen, the dank before mirk inside skipping it, corrected frames are not
neglected, pronoun at worst a construction, squeezed into road ruts
common frisbees, values peel viewers into power, parents are shocked
at this, but my own comb's bits of strips, logical space there are no
objects, compounds more serious than Kaluha, called steal not cold
steel, thought to win was advance, no lemons no melon, testate back
formation, the umber seen as this between six intervariegations, Jack
a common fellow, patch a correction to a stretched degree, my singularity
and out of place from an autograph the moulds of miles, it's a butcher
not Athens owns the aisles of grease, this is two edged sense through
all known corridors, every landscape political, the cast of characters
chart the actors' faces, fragments by part, a kidney's diameter, inchoate
storm scene between Millicent, her role in sketching, takes this length
from ligatures and the cold side for thirteen, thumbs by their yield, a
special garret at the back, eight one one three seven seven five two two,
i.e. the thickening of initial strokes to point a cursive hand that's seldom
constant, there is an open sea and chastity delays, all middle loops lift
brown, the foot in i have read them with eyes, semicolon selection, a
thorn, a wyn, an izzard, the edh, that wholesale freeze in corner sheets,

contents of a sangiad reminiscent of a finger by Ron, comma mutation, water weighed and fifteen problems, Hanoi not annoy, through body parts this stays grammatical, after midnight comes commentary, hates how the latch nears vicinity, in these parts fringes on vaticinations, titles for the coming year, plankton evaporations, an appendectomy contemporary with the spoilt version of a batch, Novrad sides reversed is Darvon, habit as half way lantern at ash boughs, begins what at bridges, a candle in latin that perfects this gulf stream, so the kettle begins it, also watching me, a visa for fatherlands plus apoplexy said aloud, completes a fiction in the manner of the peasant as dissent remains departure, essential element versus paint, the humanitarians hint samaritan hue, attack against effacement here, in the power of the plus we guarantee this real, id as a show in a major role, it takes the place of the history it's losing, computers build new archives, something diffuse set in, the concept of violence which harbours consumption, seven three two three nine, false logic extends turning sour at a lime, third world debt is when taxation matters, Spinoza indigo, four forty five Henry Moore, they are sired by wishing out of messenger to a life no longer than its zero claim, the integrity of this form is never more than each subsidiary structure, creosote behaving as the recombinant spreads veils, tense isle not tensile, a man on a bus forgets his age, allied times Artemis, a sociology of towels the way the car starts in rain, wool a commodity in trapezoid bleat whilst traps net counter to belief, the regime of a face never closes its head, slippage into mirror effect at the same time tubes glue canvas as deterrent diaries, pull up if i pull up, or a new French dressing, farm fallows function if i close my mouth to hear my eyes, delegation's oiled agents, right margins missive hats, the groceteria masks the confines of a social space, style by which stone pots boil antitypes of matter, each nude seemed planetary, vroom at the Bach, the heads above the seats with earphones indicate the cabin's full, Sherbourne, Jarvis, Church, Tahiti, the industrial prominence of flogging, so the jacinth contracts new colognes turning obsolete, the punk marine that's in his walk talking, incompatible with flooded markets, as it's happening the Olympics in Beirut, where that occurs they're orthodox in pumps, five eight seven seven nine two two, this ache of anxiety corrects itself, known programmes omega to sudden apparel, soviets not serviettes, a thumb arrives implicit, the world outside is an order within, saucepans as solitudes but the closeup notates how each factor reacts, a strategy to open growth along the networks which paralyse, in colour festucine, in salience abyssed, return this portion with your payment, equipoise to adipose, genus administrator, class mandarin, where B at not A is the practice of refluence, Toledo to Marseilles is a single red line, maple sugar real spa gum, the miles of this smell are in a sedentary schoolage, must thou and i to number six, faced fact a fallacy choking from choice, some men interpret nine memos, semiurged through bias the deaf still reason that the rational attack, in a first uncensored view of Paestrum, forks to the right suggest this too is algae, a paradise deduced from teeth nine summits too late, once rolled twice flakes itself, a nonstop samba making middles disappear, the one on the seat who orders Brecht, corrigenda from plus shrimp and pepper brochettes, but to listen breaks a bond, the cluttered cockpit of one velvet glove, versatility variety list, so we've moved to Keswick, from as low as style an urge anticipates this end, in typical pelagic mode of life, each astronaut's attraction to glabella, now it's done, Australian through spines to a moralist by thousands, relief charts in the cupboard like the goat that failed, the ptarmigan modified, a lump in motion, Capella in Auriga and still room for both, famous past words to reach conquistadora reality, the pregnant choose menopause, as something like spaniel on a bitten field, its future bifurcates that stick eats bleach, Aztec for syllable when it's happening in Chad, tense i snap pansies net, unsafe in transitory indiscretions, from Schelling a universe from Heine a poem, why this replaces pita bread, Volga not vulgar, you should protect this centre at all costs, eight precincts to five spheres, they are entering the known circumference of emotion, it's Sassenach for porridge but afterwards a sense of tripe, this work we call theme can never begin, as pleonasms swell according to the size of Catherine's bruise, the stem as steam as time distorts in clocks, aortic appetitive in the blind girl's definition of a mirror, a half block from the presidential palace and seventeen months without a job, Washington crossing the Delaware a wet crew gain Hessian strong-hold, sun to blow out, forgot in this, where two proximities converge, seven six six six three eight nine seven five five two, the listener's spoon gets tarnished, emptied to departure point as all the germs turn radical, at gunpoint agendas for a decreased workload, misery does not begin in the promenade, but loss too, is a longitude, alleluias dying cynical, how does one reach the end of language, a chicken drumstick through its see through wrap, closed for a detour, Australopithecine or Plekhanov for protestants, the nexus called influence, being is the word that writing shatters, Nature not Nietzsche,

from *An Effect of Cellophane*

what they call night in the movies was a bullet dropping in the sentence
logic undescending rain immured by the speakers cusp or jet the tissue
of a fold half opening the portrait to the thing itself distorting then
announcing there is always the discredited signet of a certain sign the
aspidistra they call the screen on every service gone before a detonation
in the engine somebody east of the sky the body nothing as the language
it spoke clipped out commentary to repeat itself a slash between the
darkness of her mouth in every sign the absence of a range and what
they call night in the movies become a knife no longer blunt or than
an inch the cygnet handle a swans neck slashed with a blade of
gynocography precision no longer the shell the grass a blade of even
body pulled the knife preventing holding back the wind as if it acted
feigned a faint allusion to the detonation in an engine what they called
the bachelor a clavichord its part of the machine drawn off an edge to
writing fragments of a pharmacy inside of what it goes beyond the
descant from a photograph a written light the surface of a sky or
common blade pulled out the mouths part of the machine in part the
repetition of itself the necessary cut or slash described discredited a
bar inside the detonation not a hinge but absence put there acting as
adjusted by the knife across an edge of sail and giving rise to sewing
folded inwardly the harbour in the dream inside a folded double seam
semantic detonation and the word allusion spelled in english through
a hinge the mouth a portrait part and then an insect doubled landing
on the shell an unhatched cygnet absent body from the writing to an
edge discredited this zoographic operation linked in turn to voice by
fullness in one visible trigger person fusion perpetration off one side
the sketch turned to terms that indicate pomeric closeness and a seal
the sygla by a virtue which as impress illustrates the move between the
fact a swan is dead and laughter or precision is a difference in fullness
set apart the fan whence spread disclosure the spatial mark points out
a leaf mould left alive a life these two which flow too unfolding doubling
out one face a multiplied transgressive blank two leaves before a space
for dying in an ordered series of expiries the swan first already there a
cut oblique one stroke as though a cygnet riddled it with skin sewn up

lacking a hole the edge bound tight upon a double fold tucked in beside
the masthead everything no longer said before the face a multiple but
fractured light caught peripheral dismembered body soundless on the
periplum what each particular had called the cite the city stood upon
organic series not as numbers swan a swarm of bees not lettuce form
all sides the hinge sound blows a pivot infiltrated set of grids as well a
sequence less remembered than remembering the exit via cut or graft
and fold still termed a seam the dress a variant of chandelier its light
in the privileged advance of face before the second split or space a
murderer might mention swan the second cygnet dying in the dance
the dancer had forgotten dying as a bird intended through itself to be
a single origin a start before addition in advance the intervention of
the fold that crumpled surface up to be an envelope effect withheld the
dancer in her topos on a paper sheet a paragraph or area the central
square of words peripheral to difference clipped line dispersed disposed
the limn as paint in pain as then that moment innumero numero
profunda we were both removed replaced within the mute machine
upon the very order of the bachelors a shot not presence still repeated
representing life before a pistol whip the ice breaking and the skin sewn
up the ear the sentence of the swan completes itself a leaped and clipped
mutation slashed along an edge of beach or page a perforation known
compared advanced the ripping silent or unheard within the bachelors
attack a dancer squared to face herself the ballerina lacking body sewn
up folded inside function doubled out into a swan the fan replaces with
a wing or arm the ice at sea the paper clipped the edge a member and
removed before translation came

Oedipus Meets the Abstract Machine

I love you too if I'm
endorsed by global information
all these little jobs of enjoyment popping up
so much ancient wisdom in marble
meanwhile, back in a poem
by Clark Coolidge™ I'm Johnny Greendoors
the clam chowder savant clean out of entelechies.
Arthur Danto enters, orders
a regular recent Chardonnay then spills
Philosophy on his corner shirt.
Guess South is East for him
in his sort of sheriff's pants
or maybe not
when toe's got a footnote for a footstool.
Smells like a huckleberry Nissan up
your nose. Nope, I'll try again
through ethical theory. Maybe
someone's elsewhere's happening out there right now.
Seems the image turns out to be
an odd text full of reception theory
and that'll throw a challenge to
the salmon samplers. Develops I'm told
out of the nomadic Synagogues, want some?
it sure beats ekphrasis in the throat.
Better ask the reindeer salesman in
next door
Now that's what I call style
and a human action explains it.

Suggestion but No Insult

"No ideas but in things"
is wrong Bill
the challenge
is how to
negotiate the shift
from
quiddity to ideation
by
a border-crossing yet
around subversions to
a fold in
measure space
caesura as transplant
and all time
to keep philosophy your friendly
insomniac
grammar born of
the hands that
question where
the wings should go

The Dangers of Poetry
(*for Italo Calvino*)

Maybe you don't like this poem or perhaps you don't want to read it
perhaps you should do something else like wash last night's dishes or
watch TV if I were you I'd try reading a good book or even start to
write one but perhaps you haven't stopped reading this poem just yet
while you're wondering what else you could read or perhaps your
interest in this poem has miraculously changed maybe you're enjoying
it or finding it a challenge or perhaps you're simply thinking it would
be a waste of precious time having read it so far to not read it to the
end or perhaps there's nothing you can do because perhaps this is a
class that you can't get out of or the start of a conference you've paid
a lot of money to attend or perhaps it's a punishment prescribed in a
minimum security prison you're now in for five or even ten years or
perhaps reading this poem has induced paralysis and you can't move
not even to blink your eyes or perhaps you believe it can't get worse
but it does get worse and you think all these thoughts again and then
compare this poem to the start of Italo Calvino's novel *If on a Winter's
Night a Traveller* and that the two might be related perhaps you think
that this poem was actually written by Calvino under the pseudonym
of Steve McCaffery and then you think that this might be the poem
Calvino didn't write but wished he had and by this time an entire week
has passed and you're still at your desk at the office because you never
went home and perhaps you couldn't have anyway because a friend
called to tell you that your house burned down and all your pets and
family burned to death because you were still reading this poem.

The Lone Ranger in Arcadia

Imagine a delicatessen subtracting at every instant
with the rhythm of a yeast infection.
Now you see it now you don't until predictably
Calypso-Fada meets Lord Kitchener
and in Tombstone

                    Polity rides mother earth

with spittoon, while reading *Lolita* in Kabul.
To simplify his thoughts on longitude
Sir Isaac Newton buys a house in
Dewsbury which Lorca insists is either Salamanca
or the hip-hop capital of Spain.

It all adds up to the meaning of "true equity"
but it sure ain't rocket science or a solar anus.

A passion for the real stops short of having it now
more honest than a fingerprint beneath the grid

        Khlebnikov refers to grasshoppers as "nodes
        of the future reflecting on their poetry as on
        reflected rays of the future cast
        by a subconscious 'I' upon
        the sky of the rational mind"

Sound, a honeycomb grown silent leaving speech
as a five-finger exercise:

1 (is mythological): the antiseptic image of Orpheus pleading with Death

2 (historical): Dr. Strangelove on his horse Enola Gay and shouting

            Hi ho Sylva!

Restricted Translation with Imperfect Level Shift (*after Basho*)

Upon a time this frog meets an unwed mother. Plot starts rain. A consideration of one pond that this makes possible. The proper name (multiplied + sterile) indeclinable in speech (momentum x sonority) expressing time, manner, condition and cause (reader = vehicle) result: degree through means.

Our man in the novel. Familiar protagonist, the tragic hero and the methodist in Jesus Christ. But also *oyster* in the subordinate system. Counts them: sanctuary seasons deposits on rock. In a sense then artificial this perception of a pond. Midnight plus the dice-throw and some ordinary rules.

Compare the fact our president has hiccups. The retinue cough in the sentence describing how the word *œsophagus* resettles to disclose mid-phrase "these ripples are an absolute dominion."

The circles mean sovereignty but disappearance where the logic of frog disembarks among its divisions. The surface norm is "plop" at least three facets swap (as stress + weight) two insects that collide.

Not a fairy tale, not metaphor, not history. Just a moment on a page a hole can crush. Something is happening to the word endless. Its anarchy is changing, its notice gloats but then retires.

Application of advancing premises to indicate a waiting. Caught like the egotist if it jumps immovable to a coloured otherwise. This was begins.

The Poem as a Thing to See

Somebody here got married in vitro
but why is mass being held
for a million televisions tendered
as deluxe facsimile ready-mades?

Perhaps a microbe's forming a Gordian knot around
uncle's breakfast demands for a family rendition
of Krummacher's story of the worm in the apple.

Shadows above the scratches of a language?

Or do we have the virus as a new archangel?

Either way it's modernity from next door
with it heavy-metal flamenco out
of focus

                    a flower and indisputably
a cryptomorphic entry into legend

(The fate of the book sealed in Flaubert's
    famous letter to Louise Colet
        but nothing
            happens
                when you

plan it

The View from Here

At 4 pm Dante starts editing his copy of
the *Anti-Dühring*
as a thought carries him to Mozart composing
his last symphony in Vienna.

Via the metapoetics of illogical space
the sound *daffodil* becomes intangible
caught in the fact that
"the rose was obsolete" is now obsolete.
The train
once standing at sentence three
demands a reader's temporality exceed
the speed of all operative systems aggregates

(Dachau however remains the single doorstep into
Shelley's essay in defence of poetry)

There are rock doves in the grass alas
combines the sum-total of allowable inter-textual
relationships to modernism and marriage (maieutic theory
must be cautious here at the teleology of Maryland
but there still is daylight savings time
in the *Booke of Margery Kempe*)

In the attic the Soviet dominant gathers artifice
anarchy embraces sentimentality as concern switches
from napalm to cholesterol and Saddam Hussein
changes his name back
to J. Alfred Prufrock.

Tyrolean Night

Characters:
( ) = O
" " = X

The machine looks conservative but gosh what a leader in experimental phonetics!

(Firdausi thought it the new *hilaritas* when he changed his name to Basho.)

Tall frogs sit on a nunuphar built by lunatics and here is the room where the mirror-playing instrument occasionally interacts with the one who writes.

"So little to remember of the years before this happened."

Periplus to a plenum but with the intellectual activity of three, not as love in the middle, but on the side of godhead approaching *in absentia* the good things of will.

(As trade so ethics.)

But here, the symbol is adequate to announce proportionality to all attending.

Concealment quickly follows Lenin lodged in the Austrian Tyrol the night it snowed in Saskatoon with nuns swarming the Vatican.

Diapason the duration of its verbal components returning each night at eleven-o-three to a thin mist over many of the earlier objectives.

Along the seacoast a temporary five-year plan versus the bruised quintessence of a Nautilus.

"It could be good to go to a play instead of staying at home and reading James Essex's *Observations on the Origin and Antiquity of round Churches; and of the Round Church at Cambridge in Particular*, small quarto 1782" when suddenly a hand appears to offer economic paradise.

The shell takes it and offers in exchange a highly innovative social history of sneezing.

Since then the burger master orders an effective system for annual economic exploitation.

"This could be wartime as once more the birds in excess of their feathers sing out proper names."

(Yours among them.)

Thinking this way creates a haunt for bohemians of an open market with its central violin explained by the fact that the man in tweed comes from Thessaly.

The petite DNA in the circular microchondria is not innate but certainly inventive in its senseless torment of the poor longshoremen.

"Let's take our next vacation in a big popular majority adjacent to the federal government building and whistle multi-corporate features as we go along."

The tiles are dark and unsophisticated in that region but each week summer returns as if the sun once shone.

Serfs rise to a rendition of addenda torn out of the final signature of Jean Francois Paul de Gondi's *Mémoires du Cardinal de Retz, de Guy Joli et de la Duchess de Nemours Nouvelle Edition* with provincial imprint fresh upon its scales.

"This brings us to a simply prodigious achievement despite the continuously successful call of an unknown requisition."

Something becomes language as the light goes out and the scientific consequence within the nature of receptacles stands finally for the source of spheres.

"It's been doing this for centuries while you were staying in the village of Erbach on the Odenwald living as a modernist from Milano sporting the word *chryselephantine* in your button-hole waiting to meet Phillip Whalen in the Preiss Hotel around the time Johann Philipp Ferdinand was born."

(But this shouldn't make you the multi-media pigeon voyeur that you want to be.)

The civil war has other effects as well as suddenness.

Starting with a prototype mistake it ends up in a practice of body fragments recollected among short-lived scenery in full flight.

(Other passengers lend money to off-shore steelyards taking two hours to lock up all the untenured faculty in the University of Geneva's Gynaecology department.)

At a rough estimate I'd say Medieval Greek doesn't have a precise term these days to describe a Futurist lexicographer.

"Why are the Alps called Catholic churches and filled with irksome vendors of second-hand sausage meat?"

Seems to me the name of a town on the west-bank of the Rhône would be equally appropriate given that the complete statement's still housed in a fire-proof structure made by the man who invented the Praetorian Guard.

"I feel I'm still trapped in the headquarters of some numerical system for Pythagorean locksmiths."

There's a chill to the night besides novel chocolate arpeggios clotting out the moon in a motionless communion some call Romanticism.

(The fact that I was writing this three days after the post office burned down is not retold in sagas from Iceland.)

There, the speaker adopts the persona of an aging Irish patriot named Desmond born of the water in Machiavelli's abridged *History of Florence* by oxen connected to a different plot.

The insurgents assume names taken from the family of a species of Nymphalidae normally found in stagnant pools around Mount Rushmore and those ideas attributed to John Dewey transliterated from Russian into the argot of some late Constitutional Assembly.

"Pity the victims destroyed by all those Judeo-Hellenic Matisse programs."

"Hopefully it will rain for some of them at a Tang Dynasty bar mitzvah party as a man is acquitted of a crime he didn't expect."

But that night at the Safari World superstition conquered the security guards and caused a sectional detour between the giraffes.

A week later D'Annunzio finishes a play written entirely in the future tense.

Set in Shenshi Province, an abandoned child called Vishnu Rhizome sings an aria in two different but simultaneous voices.

(Outside it will have been snowing on Emmanuel Swedenborg as he completes his theosophic system in a small notebook purchased somewhere between Pennsylvania and Maryland.)

At which point a pejorative grief floods a film-script about a famous twentieth-century dictator known for his unrivalled Byzantine coin collection.

(The audience bicker over the pros and cons of Henri-Martin Barzun's theory of *simultanéisme* until the muffled footsteps grow louder.)

"It could be New York or *anno domini* but read the label carefully before going back on the ice."

Ingredients such as thistle and mildew delight in the thought of triple predestination brought on by covert Neoplatonic cartels after midnight in the era of mechanical respiration.

(The records of the Royal Academy guarantee a standard ethic to some human souls and seatbelts of a quality that will sustain their overuse if art persists.)

"But I was there when the letter bomb arrived back from historical oblivion then the next thing I know is I'm swimming in a pool of plain motif anticipating consequent morality."

However the goodness of delight in others still inaugurates a complex international problem.

"Then let's blast off the glass into the laws of habitat to pose ecological and predatory problems."

(It's what cougars do best.)

There are sometimes lips that never form a mouth across the scars
and traces we call holocaust testimony.

"Perhaps memory converts them into meaning."

The flower's traces are still singable but not legible, except in the
remainder with a "cunnynge" of Dominican origin.

(Then it happens again: a fifth-rate epilepsy oozes out of the word
"rhapsodic.")

Crossing the Ganges reading Balzac doesn't get you to the tragic.

"Maudlin, granted, but the truly tragic is voiceless in Ann
Bergren's account of the originary binding of women to writing."

Animal kingdom equals America however not too close to the
White House.

"The trap of course presumes a loose enclosure for any missing
or vagrant texts such as Tiphaigne de la Roche's *Giphantia: or, A
View of What has Passed in the World* the last two words of which
are translated in the next line from Arabic when suddenly specific
diversity restraint ratios are ruled a constant among the Maskes at
Ludlow."

Intense ribbed patterning suggests the footnotes entered via a
calcite soap solution.

Through an Arctic winter the leg-pendulum describes a greater
arc, its vortex modified by fusel oil dropped from paraffin.

Form falls (for a time) into sentient amino-programmes following a statistical bridge connecting the few remaining Cartesian mind-grids working to monopolize known multiplicities in order to establish the birth of the thinking object.

(A co-ordinate range inaugurates the requisite Glossary of Greek fishes.)

Volatility Buddha architectures prove echo's the refusal to be twin.

"Don't worry, this facilitates panopticality as a cyclical non-numerical avenue to time."

Fanacalo esperanto down the cobalt mines gives way to knowledge that a library exists in which the front door's in the United States and all the books are in Canada.

"It's needless to add that the theological concept of a fall facilitates the origin of sexual difference and history."

(Pictorial structure from foreground to distance in a late work of Andrea Mantegna's produces tandem retinal repetitions, but a conflict emerges in the freedom = negativity equation.)

The problem pertaining to angelic annunciations is the echo options allowed the addressee.

"A practice of prayer has its hazards: wounds in water obvious to a thinker."

And here the spider silently expires, rectangular, in stories of unravelling where allegory passes into general semiosis.

A little later the car starts at the door to the room of the ideogram for "Grand Panorama" where someone has written out the Law of the Question as it occurs in Michael Dalton's *The Country Justice*, 1690, bound in full contemporary calf.

(Previously a neo-mannerist concept of discontinuous history guaranteed translated investment at a higher level of profit than simply "good.")

My name is Ben F, but not in this poem where the closest exit may be an entrance to the anechoic nerve bleep sutures.

"This is the place where volatility can happen as smectic marles collect in passing a coded potter's rule across a pebble powder to the waiting eyes."

Contiguous to a swan's death and at night with a weak demographic behind them demoiselle cranes fly over the Hymalayas into their National Geographic dream.

A house decides to reverse its plan and become its own impossible event in current theories of the leisure class.

(Across the pain of a pin in the head the day has finally invented God.)

Instantly, as polymorph or gerund, a small mutant yeast colony cuts off the oxidative phosphorylation supplies destined for the Alte Pinakothek in Munich causing a lion hunt to start as oil on canvas.

"It is here that enthusiasm tends to generalize the tradition of tufted trees caught in the Gaspard Dughet landscapes popularized by the Chatelaine engravers."

The full moon rushes into rouge and precisely six years later a part of *L'Allegro* gets interpreted that escapes William Empson's comprehension in a Bangor toyshop.

(Elsewhere in the third-period of extra time a Scandinavian hockey player conceives a successful method of cloning a dog with a silent bark.)

Owing to the heavy rain each word means precisely what it signifies in *The Cottage Hymn-Book*, enlarged edition and suitable for both private worship and public use.

(But I wouldn't start a bar room quarrel over it, spell-check and the banks will do it for you.)

"We have a bibliography of worlds to read and H. von Pückler-Muskau's *Briefe eines Verstorbenen aus Frankreich*, Munich, 1830 is our guide!"

A Map

is a schedule
or Mogadishu comprising
phraseology in defeat.

The length of shadows this employs
to shrink its resurrected problem
sober, but joined to
a popular legacy
a tongue found tense below
the principle angle of shrapnel.

Later
being extant through anorgasmic infiltration,
bodies emerge in Spain to situate as protocols
then reinscribe as stanzas in a theorem.

Ice recollecting is description now
a growth conceded to
the February mental pattern arrived,
at last, in parachute complexity on T H A S
as a line
cornered by all the death-squads
outside a well-kept stalemate.

Correlata for a Cryptogram

It looks like California outside
the mudslides of pure mascara
but it's been said before:
you can't give an inch a new nail.

Curious, however,
the return to the mystic writing pad
for just the briefest scribble
of top-right Celtomania.

Around these parts
simultaneity in claws is
the puma's best form of disappearance
just follow the arrow from the national diagonals
to reach the correlata for a cryptogram
around the throat of America

the way milk escapes the entire history
of its blackness.

The Logic of Six

97632. Trajectories to seek a lexicon and an inference. Ask so a choir falls due to the federation of a sentence. 415 eleven 12. Radio to air. The collapse to coincidence on the nine dice sides. Fifteen 13. This represents the fifth. An 8. I have said it.

To the context alone a vertical horizon might petition diagonally its own grace notes as an episodic shift. Chapter twenty-four. This represents my having said so. I am saying the 6th. But not always as ready. The figurative would seem aware of a trick deployed a couple of lines before. So I don't say this. 1158 fifty-six 32 2612 does not represent the tenth. Or any number. 7. 5. 3 now. The figures speak so this must have said it.

A paragraph administers five drops of liquid to an I. Oddly six even 9. Petitioned diagonally as an episodic shift this forms a vertical scalar of 6 between three. A figural imbalance does not say the same. I see or it says. This most certainly becomes the fifth. 806 teen. The last of the allegories.

Having nothing to do with anything above. Twenty 1. xviii. A vertical smooth and unstriated precipitate of event. The reclined decline to a 6ty3. This saying collapses into the coincidence of the nine dice sides. Not yet as above them. Fifteen 1163. This agent is beckoning some logic of reception. 18 perverse and somewhere nine indestructible. There rests the saying. In an effort to stay smooth administering a vertical horizon to the eleventh of all these numbers. xxx76xiivii. A lexicon as an inter-ference and so acquired the past fails. Signs of this as residue. Nine (9) six (5) five (3) one (1).

Somehow this credits a missing surplus as a genealogy that limits growth. 8733599. Mixed passages to the negative. Of what. This besides is now a beckoning. If what. There rests a seeing. Posthumous birth before the principle attests. Of an end soon.

For 6 what 8. A paragraph upon this and positioned it might seem diagonally through an inference toward that lexicon below it. xvi. I have placed it as the ninth.

Volume ten is a teleology to limit breathing. Surplus still petitioned.

Partitioned 7 thirteen 8tyi. One 12 like all the rest. The other way around a4ords seventeen treatises. Paragraph seven. Around what. The platform might mean sense. I had just taken place when this was already happening. Radio to air not said. Six. Writing with atoms and periods. Seven. Not then. Eight. Where then. The 5. Not where.

Along the apparatus of a line exists a foreign policy for words. Some sixty fives. Another 92. This once represented a twelfth of all of this. I have said that. The strength of the probable nine dice sides. Translation supplied by the father founder. Or rather a squandering of space. A one-way pesticide. Not here. The twenty-two but a 3. Not when I have said this. A one to the three. Another 35.

Thus the 5th part of any language. 91997. The numbers when multiplied. The remnants literal. Litotes of creditor six to debtor seventy-one. By the imposition of a contractual property two reads as my fifteen again. You are seventy-three now. Alliance of a choir with the federation of all sentences. Everything above that is wrong. Out take in accurate. I have said it before. That the nine becomes another two. In this form the trajectories might change to represent that fifth as fifteen. Subject. In so far as when disappearing in the 20. This appearance in a six.

Trajectories through five a lexicon and seven. And so a 3 falls due to the federation of the fifth. Radio to air. The collapse to sevens on the nine dice sides. Fifteenth thirteen to represent the six. Eight. Seven has said it. To the context thus a vertical thirteen petitioned diagonally as an episodic four. 9 keeps saying the fifth. But not always in eleven. The figurative accordingly would seem aware of ix deployed a couple of sevens before. So vii doesn't say this. Or any number. Allegory seven for 531. The numbers speak and that has said this.

Paragraph 19 administers 5 drops of liquid to a one. 4 8 eleven 6 9. This figural imbalance doesn't say this time. Six. One. One sees or one says. This most certainly becomes the sixth. 66. Sixteen.

Having a different seventeen to do with thirty 8 above. 21. Eighteen vertical sixes on an unstriated precipice of elevens. The recline to 16. 6ty three. This is twice seven. 1460. This eighty 7 collapses into the coincidence of nine dice threes. Not as above them. xv eleven vi 3. This below it is beckoning to four as a logic of numbers both perverse and 16 indestructible. There rests the ii.

Five 221 seventeen 12 vi. It's this effort to stay six at 6 that administers a vertical eleven to the 5th of all these incidents. Episode 376137. A twenty vi and an interference which so acquired the nine falls to three in this residue. Nine six 6 five. A mixed seventeen here with the negative. Of what. 4ty iii beside fifty 6 when beckoning. Of ten. There rest the six. Posthumous 12 before the seventy six attestations. Of an eleven soon. For six. A paragraph upon this and petitioned it would seem diagonal again through eighty six thoughts towards a ninety 5 below it. Five 3 xvi. I have placed the eight. Ten in the fifth.

A thirty-three to limit the last 18. 70 still petitioned. Partitioned 73 eighty one one 12 like the two twice removed. The other five above ground. Seventeen. Four. Around what. This new 78 might mean extended sense. I had just taken five when six already was nineteen. Fifty 5 five iii seven. Twenty eight to three not nine. Writing with sevens and 6teens. Plus seven. Not ten. Eight. Where then. The five. Not five.

Some eights. The four. One three. This apparatus for a six exists as a foreign eight to words. A sixty five at last. The 92. This represents the fifth. I have said six. The strength of the thirteen nine dice sevens. Translation supplied by the father of forty five. A sixteen deleted. Or rather a squandering of five. The one two pesticide not twelve when I said six. A one some twos. Nineteen thirty-v.

Just a fifth seventeenth of a language demultiplied in eighteen figurals. Creditor six to seventeenth 17. By the imposition of a contractual demand upon allegory ninety two. Sixteen seeing six before it. The nine becoming another two. In all of this the trajectories might change to re-seventeenth the fifth. A 15 them some sevens. Or any number. Subject. 17. In so six as four when. This 20th appearance. In a six.

Nine 7 (6) 3 (two.) Trajectories to a v a 17 and a 7. And so a III falls 6 to the eighteen sides of the 5th. Seventy-nine chapters to paragraph VII. The line collapses into limited phrase groups on the IX dice sides. xv. 13. This fails to represent the fifth. x not always eleven. The xxvI would seem aware of a nine deployed a couple of sevens before. 19 seven doesn't say it's IX. Or any number. Allegory seven. Phrase 5. Part III. The thirteens speak and xI has thought it earlier.

A fifty (2) two (50) administers five sevens of xIX to an eight. Four 8 eleven vI six IX. This numerical imbalance does not remain a five. Six. Then one. And previously one six inside two nines. This is certainly xvII becoming the fifth outside of 80 different attempts. Three at last with thirty-eight deletions to the side. xxI. 18. A twelve 6 and an unstriating xII into eleven. The fifteen is a 16. Sixty isn't 3. vII remains seven. Fourteen reaches 60. This secondary eighty of the set collapses into the xxxvII sections of the 9 dice fives. xLv remain above them. The 15 in eleven the vI in III. Nineteen chapters below a start that's beckoning. The logic of six pervades perverse and indestructible as four of ten of the remaining trajectories in two.

First Vico Meditation

O

Dime

O

Cross-section of aorta

O

Aerial view of Coliseum

O

Tiger's nipple

O

Eye drop

O

Mirror

Second Vico Meditation

O
Rent a Centre

O
Sell a Hole

Digital Poetics

To read this poem in French press 1, in German press 2, in Spanish press 3, in English press 4. To read an index of all reviews, books and articles written about this poem press 5. For previous readers' opinions of this poem press 6. To read all variorum drafts in facsimile manuscript of this poem press 7. To read the final proof copy before publication press 8. To read the first printed version of this poem press 9. For a total line count press 10. For a total word count press 11. For a total character count press 12. For a list of all colleges and universities where this poem is taught press 13. For a list of anthologies in which this poem has appeared press 14. For a photograph and biography of the author press 15. To read all musical adaptations of this poem press 16. To read a dramatic version of this poem press 17. To read the libretto of and score to the operatic version of this poem press 18. For a list of bookstores where all books containing this poem are currently available press 19. For a list of stores where the CD version is available press 20. To read a different poem by this author press 21. To read a different poem by another author press 22. To read a shorter poem by this author press 23. To read a longer poem press 24. To read a better poem press 25. To read an on-line version of this poem press 26. To repeat this menu press 27. To read a commentary on these commands and a critical discussion of the social phenomenon of interpellation press 28. To read a commentary on these commands and their relation to Vico's cyclical theory of history press 29. To read a comparison of this touch-tone method to John Dee's Enochian tables press 30. For more information on John Dee's Enochian Tables press 31. To read factual information about John Dee press 32. To read information on Enoch press 33.

Prior to Meaning

(Lost listening to paint)

(a whiter Odalisque inside
encounter's notation)

(the specific instances of angels or tugboats
in a struggle

so absent over surface is

the stream that's there)

connoisseurship flooded
in saintly deixis

a contradiction
to a proof

(that i had brought you joy and you
returned it as a coming

outside)

historical relations are
the travellers' tongues

on this thursday, or december

between a manger
on a patio

(and having lost a destiny

to feel that dream to need)

Afterword

The 1980s proved an important decade for me. In 1986, my critical writings from 1973 through 1986 appeared collectively as *North of Intention* in a joint Canadian and American venture. It was also a decade in which some of my most substantial poetic texts appeared: the collaborative *Legend* (1980), the aphoristic *Knowledge Never Knew* (1983), *Evoba* (my poetic rescension of Wittgenstein's *Philosophical Investigations*, 1987), and *The Black Debt* (1989), whose two lengthy components ("Lag" and "An Effect of Cellophane") realized my own poetics of recombination and phrase propulsion (in deliberate contrast to the New Sentence). The year 1988 was marked by the tragic passing of my dear friend and colleague bpNichol. During the two decades sampled here in *Verse and Worse*, I published eleven poetry titles through nine different presses based in four different countries.

I mention these facts to underscore some fundamental proclivities in my writing that should be evident in the material republished here: a stridently anglophonic non-nationalism, a rejection of an ego-based poetry, and a deep commitment to formal innovation. Notions of "identity," "self," and "subject" have never been important factors in my writing. This is not to say that these do not inform my work, but that such matters have never been a focus or pre-occupation. As a white heterosexual male, matters of identity are what one tries to escape and I've found my persistent commitment to collaboration (critical and creative) a mainstay to non-unity and decentredness.

Georges Perec has always provided me with an inspirational model for writing and publishing: diversify, make each publication entirely different from the former. (As such, a publication such as Ron Silliman's *The Alphabet* is utterly alien to my sensibility.) My friend bp constantly harangued me to gather together my former, current, and future poetic writings into a single work, *The Abstract Ruin*, and to make it "Panel III" of *Carnival*. This I have never done. However, I concur with him on one important credo: that those discrete units we call "poems"—gathered into those larger units we call "books" and sometimes partitioned into "decades"—are false discontinuities in that indescribable and unpredictable ontological praxis known as writing. I certainly do not think that any writing (be it Charles Olson's or Christine de Pisan's) divides rationally or purposefully into decades and such artificial chronologizing impedes as much as it facilitates a pleasurable (or otherwise) encounter.

In arriving at parameters for this section, I decided on a number of exclusions. First and foremost, none of my collaborative work is represented; hence, sections from the collaborative sound-text scores of the Four Horsemen and my part-published but ongoing collaboration with Karen Mac Cormack (*From a Middle*) do not appear. Equally, none of my collaborative and solo sound work is represented (an ideal *Selected* would include an accompanying CD). My visual, concrete, and non-linear poetry is similarly absent, although samples of this can be found in *Seven Pages Missing* and on the Coach House website. There are however two exceptions: the two Vico meditations can justifiably be considered "visual" poems, although I personally regard them as conceptual; the poems from *Paradigm of the Tinctures* are part of a collaborative work with British poet Alan Halsey, a collaboration in which Alan supplied stunning visual collages that match (often in odd ways) my own accompanying poems. As printed here they give a false presentation of the dialogism between word and image, but I judge them to stand as independent texts. These parameters were agreed upon with Darren and we arrived at a somewhat visually orthodox gathering of texts with prose blocks and ragged-right line endings providing the dominant visual impression. But hopefully the poems display a somewhat non-linear thinking.

After my theorizing of Language poetics and the resultant poems, or rather creative manifestations (in such works as *Theory of Sediment*, 1991, and *The Black Debt*, 1989), my work took a philosophical turn in the late 1980s in the sense that the syncretism it always seeks shifted from socio-linguistic critique toward an inclusion of post-structural and post-phenomenological adaptations. Preeminently I sought poetic applications of primarily philosophical ideas. For instance, in "Lag" I applied Lyotard's theory of "phrase universes" as outlined in his book *The Differend*, as well as Deleuze and Guattari's notion of "becoming," to a specific "becoming meaning" that reveals itself in a festive expenditure of persistent yet loose connecting phrases. A common site of inquiry in many of the poems is not only how meaning is produced but how meaning is lost, or rather how poems can stage for the reader the experience of a risk of the loss of meaning. There are several techniques exploited to this effect: phrase propulsion I've mentioned above, but others include the logical shifts and semantic gaps consequent to the paratactic structure of a piece like "Tyrolean Night," and a wilful "misapplication" of a specific type of discourse to a form for which it was not intended (as in "Digital Poetics").

I've always retained from my reading of Charles Olson's "Projective Verse" one important precept: the structural importance of kinetics to the revelation and disappearance of meaning (his notions of "breath" and "energy" do not factor in my work, but the importance of kinetics does). Speed is essential to the structure of "Lag" and the finite recombinations that make up "An Effect of Cellophane."

Another element informing much of this work is a "slippage to indeterminacy." Barthes's and Lacan's notion of the free-floating signifier strikes me as offering a fecund potential for poetics. Saussure too, in his rethinking of the old relation of word to thing as a new relation (and one entirely within language) of signifier and signifier, suggested the potential of detachment and a linguistic economy of emancipated signifiers in the search for a non-representational poetry. I've long felt the rejection of representation crucial to any investigation into styles of poetic thinking. What constitutes such a discretion? Not entirely the abandonment of logic but certainly the freedom to a certain capriciousness in its application, arrived at through a tactical linking of words into propositional units.

I recall puzzling one member in an audience at a reading I did several years ago in London, England, with the phrase "disambiguated geese." To his question "What does it mean?" I answered, "It doesn't mean anything, but it allows you to think and in so doing you experience a fresh, perhaps novel juxtaposition of two common words." I think this hones in on the quintessential significance in Barrett Watten's notion of total syntax: a transposition of neologism from the invention of new words to the invention of new phrases and propositional units. Examples of this linguistic-cognitive phenomenon populate the selections in this book; they are examples of my commitment to that perhaps masochistic hortation of Modernism to make it new.

But innovation for its own sake is, like art for art's sake, ultimately otiose. Kenneth Goldsmith's and Tan Lin's recent claims on behalf of unoriginality and uncreativity are major interventions in the contemporary avant-garde that need to be taken seriously. But they too partake in a legacy of negative poetics that starts in anglophone literature as early as the Preface to the second edition of Wordsworth and Coleridge's *Lyrical Ballads*. Bold innovation is immediately co-opted into a patinated rhetoric of supercession that gets one nowhere beyond the ephemeral titillations of fashion. I prefer the other narrative that revisions the avant-garde as a storehouse of available and cumulative techniques deemed viable and adaptable to the urgencies of the present. Poetry won't change the world but might render the world rethinkable. This is not a Utopian inclination but a move within a multiplicity of dreams, agendas, mistakes, and arrogances. It is a poetics of promiscuity envisioned as a tactic. I adopt a chiasmic view of history that's partly Eliotian and partly Benjaminian: the present contemporarizes the past as much as the contemporary is historicized by the past. Any worthwhile poetic must be historically rigorous and admit the capricious power of the anachronism.

A serious rethinking of the lyric and aesthetics in general is evident too in this selection. I believe Jeremy Prynne derived from the poetry of George Meredith the phenomenon of a dizzying display of terminology that nonetheless is stabilized by a feeling of surety, of "lyric" anchor. I won't call this "voice" and thereby open a Pandora's box of problems, but I will venture to call it architected style. It is style that offers a refuge for the self and it is evident in the paradox of Eliot's modernist poetics of impersonality that in so many ways has dominated the contemporary from Cage and MacLow to Goldsmith and Bök. Style reveals the individual behind it, bringing word and flesh together in a writing that, of necessity, interpenetrates a world. My "style" is evident in all the poems in this volume and my "life" informs them insofar as my reading constitutes a major component of both my writing and my life. I like to think of lyric not as a historically defined genre but an atmosphere in which its problems, contradictions and aporia play themselves out. There is a distinctly "lyric" quality in several of the poems in *Verse and Worse,* but in being present it is problematized. Think of lyric as a certain weight of language gained through the ineluctable sedimentation of the poet's medium: words added to a specific method of construction. It is a neutral constant that allows the operative presence of illogicality without the evidence of schizophrenia or surrealism; it permits a defamiliarized experience to be digested without disgust.

And let's not forget humour and the simple pleasure of a laugh. Poets should not take themselves too seriously as politicians or world-changers (leave that to the Pol Pots, Stalins, Indira Gandhis, Margaret Thatchers, and Jesus Christs of the planet). Mina Loy envisaged a wonderful portmanteau of practical science and linguistic innovation she called "the laboratory of the word" and dropped Gertrude Stein in it. Laboratories are used for dissection and transmutations, anatomizations and alembications. I like to think of both these uses as operative within the poems that make up *Verse and Worse.* Many years ago in an interview published in *Sagetrieb,* Robert Creeley distinguished my work from that of other Language poets by the unrelenting presence of humour. That state of the induced laugh has been adequately philosophized from Bergson to Bataille, its revolutionary power installed inside advanced counter-insurgencies against the hegemony of the Logos. I'm glad it's present in this book: the induced chuckle that propels ego into orbit and relativizes most reality and all pretense. Its elder sister of course is satire, that almost defunct *telos* of writing that dominated and defined the eighteenth century. The lampoon seems to have shifted ground from poetry to late-night television. Most poems here do not include the joke-as-such (eager readers will have to wait for my new book *Dark Ladies* for that), but it does embrace humour as a key element in the reader–writer relation.

Humour in poetry is partly an effect of language's lability—its autopoeitic inclination to excess, multiplicity and indecidability. David McKettrick and Adrian Johns have each traced the entire history of printing until 1830 as the triumph of instability and uncertainty empirically undercutting that multiple modularity on which print knowledge and certainty is based. These poems exploit a significatory potential that is curiously in concordance with that history. The fifteen years spent on "accidental research" that saw light in *Imagining Language* reinforced for the poet in me a fundamental dynamic of linguistic signs: not to fixity and repeatable designation, but to capriciousness, volatility and the archaic dynamic of the swerve away from a norm. That, in a nutshell, is creed and testimony to the fact that my true muse is neither negativity nor Beatrice but the clinamen, the divine goddess of the swerve. Curves, inclinations, the disrupted-but-not-severed linear flow, are the proto-poetic dynamics behind *Verse and Worse,* and they connect it to that notorious and glorious minor science of modernism: 'Pataphysics, Alfred Jarry's science of imaginary solutions.

Let me delineate a few instances of my own 'pataphysical work reprinted in the present volume. "The Dangers of Poetry," "Apologia Pro Vita Sua" and the earlier "Restricted Translation with Imperfect Vowel Shift (after Basho)": these attempt to present a poetry modeled on the two fundamental laws of 'Pataphysics: the clinamen or swerve (already mentioned) and the syzygy, an astronomical term denoting the momentary conjunction of two opposites. I've long felt that Jarry's *fin de siècle* definition both anticipates and exceeds Reverdy's theory of the surrealist image. (Breton's rehabilitation of the sentence into the avant garde after the momentous move to words in freedom marks the most conservative moment within the history of vanguard modernism.)

Moreover, Jarry's science embraces a trans-disciplinarity that has been a lasting influence on my own swerving poetics which advocate the staging and merging of variant and frequently oppositional discourses. Many poems in *Verse and Worse* mix vocabularies of science, philosophy, linguistics and other allegedly non-poetic discourses into a multiplicity that hopefully mirrors some conditions of our age, an updating so to speak of Robert Duncan's brave envisioning of a symposium of the whole. Others slide a renegade content into an orthodox format (the samples from "The Entries" for instance that offer 'pataphysical [re]definitions of familiar words within the stylistic protocols of a dictionary.) Rather than Duncan's dream of a holism, these poems celebrate multiplicity in a poetic parallel to Jean-Luc Nancy's ontological call for a "being singular plural." I will refrain from elaborating this into a passive liberal multiculturalism and the kind of bureaucratic tokenism that has reduced the Canada Council awards and grant criteria into a farcical myopia to singular histories and geographies, and insist that acknowledgement of multiplicity and difference must further carry an acknowledgement of contestation, *agon* and whatever historically remains of the system of the dialectic. In this I am a firm supporter of Marjorie Perloff's brave and pioneer campaigns against judgment being clouded by the politically correct.

Language too inflects social material (a point insisted on by Bruce Andrews), and the poems selected for *Verse and Worse* do not represent an abnegation from a world albeit mediated by and constructed through language. There *is* a world outside the text and hopefully the poems included diffract, refract and to a certain extent enact that world. Hence, the verbal markers of historical contingence like Mogadishu, penned during the first crisis in Somalia and now surprisingly revivified. I exploit the possibility for proper names to inflect particularities and historical moments but used this way, as markers of currency, fall victim to the fallacy of eternal relevance. This is the fate of Alexander Pope's great poem *The Dunciad,* whose Gildens, D'Urfeys and Cibbers now sound like rejected moments in *Finnegans Wake.* Yet the poem remains eminently readable and comprehensible without the prosthetic aid of biographical glosses.

Let me end with a lament and a seduction. There are poems that I'm sad cannot be included because of length. "Teachable Texts" (an excerpt of which appears in this collection) is a favourite of mine and a poem that I think stands the test of time, likewise "Poetry in the Pissoir." Both are available (theoretically in earlier formats). I withheld poems from the *Basho Variations* and *Every Way Oakly* (my homolinguistic translations of poems in Stein's *Tender Buttons*) as a courtesy to my publisher, the brave Jay MillAr, in the hope that sales of his editions will reap largesse. Finally, a thanks (as always) to my wife Karen Mac Cormack, who interrupted her own projects to help me make an initial choice of texts, and finally to Darren Wershler, whose robust and insightful comments and choices resulted in the present selection. But (most significantly) I extend my appreciation of his ongoing commitment to the importance of my work in all its forms.

Buffalo, 29 July 2009

Acknowledgements

Excerpts from Lag, *An Effect of Cellophane, Theory of Sediment*, and *Teachable Texts*, plus "Restricted Translation with Imperfect Level Shift (after Basho)," "The Curve to Its Answer," "The Entries," "The Logic of Six," "Prior to Meaning," and "A Theory of the Lyric," are the same versions that appear in *Seven Pages Missing Volume One: Selected Texts 1969–1999* (Coach House Books, 2001) and *Seven Pages Missing Volume Two: Previously Uncollected Texts 1968–2000* (Coach House Books, 2002). Thanks to Christina Palassio, Evan Munday, and Alana Wilcox for their assistance with this material. Special thanks to Nathan Baker for locating and organizing the archival files.

"Tyrolean Night," "Apologia pro vita sua," and "The Dangers of Poetry (for Italo Calvino)" are from *Slightly Left of Thinking: Poems, Texts and Post-Cognitions* (Chax Press, 2008). Thanks to Charles Alexander for making it possible for them to appear here.

"A Child's History of Rhetoric Caught as It Happens," "Ephemera," "Oedipus Meets the Abstract Machine," "The Lone Ranger in Arcadia," "The Poem as a Thing to See," "The View from Here," and "Correlata for a Cryptogram" are from *Paradigm of the Tinctures*, with illustrations by Alan Halsey (Granary Books, 2007).

Steve McCaffery would like to thank all of the journals, magazines, and small presses that first published his poetry, both the works that appear in this volume and elsewhere.

Cover photo by Steve McCaffery, of books in the library of Steve McCaffery and Karen Mac Cormack, Buffalo, N.Y., 2009.

lps Books in the Laurier Poetry Series
Published by Wilfrid Laurier University Press

Steve McCaffery *Verse and Worse: Selected and New Poems of Steve McCaffery* 1989–2009, edited by Darren Wershler, with an afterword by Steve McCaffery • 2010 • xiv + 76 pp. • ISBN 978-1-55458-188-7

Don McKay *Field Marks: The Poetry of Don McKay*, edited by Méira Cook, with an afterword by Don McKay • 2006 • xxvi + 60 pp. • ISBN-10: 0-88920-494-2; ISBN-13: 978-0-88920-494-2

Al Purdy *The More Easily Kept Illusions: The Poetry of Al Purdy*, edited by Robert Budde, with an afterword by Russell Brown • 2006 • xvi + 80 pp. • ISBN-10: 0-88920-490-X; ISBN-13: 978-0-88920-490-4

Fred Wah *The False Laws of Narrative: The Poetry of Fred Wah*, edited by Louis Cabri, with an afterword by Fred Wah • 2009 • xxiv + 78 pp. • ISBN 978-1-555458-046-0